THE SEVEN DAYS OF ST. NICKLAUS

A Christmas Story for Dog Lovers

outskirts
press

The Seven Days of St. Nicklaus
A Christmas Story for Dog Lovers
All Rights Reserved.
Copyright © 2022 Dale K. Haas
v1.0

The opinions expressed in this manuscript are solely the opinions of the author and do not represent the opinions or thoughts of the publisher. The author has represented and warranted full ownership and/or legal right to publish all the materials in this book.

This book may not be reproduced, transmitted, or stored in whole or in part by any means, including graphic, electronic, or mechanical without the express written consent of the publisher except in the case of brief quotations embodied in critical articles and reviews.

Outskirts Press, Inc.
http://www.outskirtspress.com

ISBN: 978-1-9772-4877-0

Cover Image by Dale K. Haas

Outskirts Press and the "OP" logo are trademarks belonging to Outskirts Press, Inc.

PRINTED IN THE UNITED STATES OF AMERICA

Table of Contents

Foreword i

Day One: Christmas Eve 2005 1

Day Two: Christmas Day 2005 23

Day Three: Monday 12/26/05 29

Day Four: Tuesday, December 27 39

Day Five: Wednesday, December 28 45

Day Six: Thursday, December 29 50

Day Seven: Friday, December 30 76

Postlogue 89

St. Nicklaus at six weeks old.

Foreword

I dedicate this book to all those people in my life that influenced me and my love for animals over the past 60 plus years. In particular, thanks to my parents and my nine siblings for the soft spot in their hearts and their inherent love for God's creatures. To all my brothers and sisters who couldn't turn their backs on any animal that might be in need of help. The array of stray animals that were brought home, or showed up and became nourished, nurtured and ultimately loved by the whole family was utterly astounding. From Patch, the first family dog, that I grew up with, and had been rescued as a puppy by my brother Dean from a local sanitary landfill. To Nip, my very "own" first dog, to Timmy, my Mother's talking parakeet, chickens, bunnies, mice and to an endless stream of orphaned cats who knew a good thing (namely my Mother) when they stumbled across one. I'm convinced that these animals and the love poured upon each and every one of them were major factors behind my love of animals and my obsessive desire to rescue any of them in need. This story is just one chapter in a much larger book on the animals to whom I've provided some assistance throughout my life. It's a small example of the love created that comes about when two lives intersect, if brought together through nothing other than mere co-incidence, fate or even more likely, the Grace of God.

Day One

Christmas Eve 2005

Christmas of 2005 started off like any other in Jacksonville, Florida, after all the wrapping of presents, packing the car, and driving the four and a half hours from Aiken, South Carolina to share the holidays with the in-laws and the Jacksonville family.

As usual, the car was packed to the hilt, every square inch used to the maximum. My father-in-law, Clyde, always marveled at my prowess of packing a car. Admittedly, it is a pretty strong ability and many times a true engineering feat.

Upon arriving in Jacksonville and after unloading the car, hauling luggage, presents, baked goods, coolers, and golf clubs, I finally settled into an easy chair to unwind from the craziness and stress of a holiday drive on I-95.

I was relaxing in the den watching golf or college football on television. The women (my wife Teresa and my Mother-in-law) were already gathered in the kitchen rattling pots and pans sharing holiday recipes and catching up. Clyde had just headed out to the grocery store. For some reason this daily ritual appears to be recurring event comprised of three or four trips a day for retirees. The stash of groceries is barely unloaded when something was either forgotten or didn't make the original list requiring a return trip. I don't know if it's just another chance to get out of the house or more likely a great place to socialize and interact with other mankind.

Clyde was a retired grocer whose shopping includes as much analysis and inspection of the store, meats, produce, and grocery prices as it does checking off items on his shopping list. His trips usually ended in a full report on the escalating (outrageous) prices of food these days or a performance review of the produce or meat department or the store management and/or staff.

My favorite mother-in-law (MFMIL) is the paramount cook and loves nothing more than to shop for that next great southern living recipe in waiting. I think her excursions consist primarily of helping those lost souls (especially the men) wandering the aisles in search of all those items on their shopping list than truly doing any serious grocery shopping of her own. Whatever the reason, on most days at least while we are visiting, it is a three or four time a day ritual of excursions to and from the grocery.

If there was one major challenge for Christmas this year, it was the fact that MFMIL was dealing with a broken ankle. She suffered the break while, of all things, decorating the Christmas tree when she twisted her leg the wrong way and broke two bones in her ankle. I never thought of decorating the Christmas tree as a contact sport but sure enough she had the cast on her leg to prove it. Consequently, she was destined to spend the entire holiday back and forth between crutches and a wheelchair.

For her, cooking Christmas dinner for 10-15 family and friends has always been an extravagant affair, but doing so from a wheelchair brought with it many additional challenges to overcome. But she did her usual masterful job of cooking an elaborate meal while wheeling herself around the kitchen, her bum leg kneeling on the seat of the wheelchair and pushing herself to and fro like a thirteen year old kid on a skateboard. Even in that "debilitated state" she didn't miss orchestrating every meal, especially this Christmas which was just beginning to take shape as one of the most remarkable and memorable Christmas' any of us would ever encounter and certainly would never forget.

Suddenly my father-in-law came barging back in through the kitchen door all excited and said, "Dale get your hat and coat and come out here." It wasn't until I gathered my things and got outside that he started to explain when he was backing out of the driveway, he almost hit a dog that ran behind his car. Fortunately, he spotted her in the rear view mirror and stopped in time. He stopped the car and got out to make sure everything was all right when their neighbor informed him there was also a puppy following the female dog that just proceeded to run off and abandon the little one. The tiny puppy, suddenly scared and alone, found refuge on their neighbor's front porch trying desperately to disguise (camouflage) himself between a row of potted plants and the front wall of the house. I guess seeing me all these years with the two dogs we already own, Clyde thought this little puppy's best chance at survival might begin with me.

I'll never lose that image of that tiny puppy hunkered down behind those plants hoping that I didn't see him hiding there in his newly found haven of safety. It's hard for me to fathom the anxiety running through his mind and tiny body at that very moment. His mother having just run off, leaving him to his own survival and now confronted by all these large strange creatures looming over him ready to do who knows what. Not knowing what kind of dog this was or really being able to tell just how big he was, I wasn't sure if he was going to take my hand off or lick me to death. My mind was suddenly racing. It's amazing what runs through your mind in a matter of nanoseconds at times like those. Is this a wild dog? Who knows what diseases he may be carrying? What happens if he decides I'm going to harm him and he strikes first by biting me in self- defense, or will he be docile merely out of fright?

Fortunately, when I reached behind the plant and picked him up, it was much more the latter. The little ball of golden fluff, although filthy and flea ridden just melted into my arms and nuzzled up tight against my neck like he had been doing it forever. The more I looked at him, the more I realized "forever" couldn't have been much more than four, five, maybe six weeks old at the most. He was such a little peanut. He was a stunningly beautiful puppy but I could not get over just how tiny he was.

I was amazed at how calm and comfortable he seemed in my arms as we walked back to the house. I'm not sure he ever moved from the first time he nestled that fuzzy little head and cold, wet nose into the crook of my neck until we got back into the house. When we hit the kitchen door and the ladies got their first glimpse of this little fellow, the commotion was only the beginning of the magical ride we and the little guy were about to embark upon. That includes all of those people lucky enough and blessed enough to be sprinkled with a bit of his magic pixy dust.

We decided to put him into their fenced backyard for safe holding while I went in search of his mother. After securing the puppy in the backyard I ventured out across the neighborhood in search of the puppy's mother. I wondered up and down the streets, whistling and calling out in the hope of getting a dog to bark and maybe find the mother. Block after block, I found nothing. I did come about two Golden Retrievers playing with their owners out in their yard and not knowing what breed of dog this puppy was, I thought it could certainly be a Golden. I disturbed the family basketball game and asked the folks if they were missing a puppy. Unfortunately they were not and neither of their golden retrievers had any puppies.

After walking a few more blocks and coming up empty, I was a few blocks from my in-law's home walking along the St. John's River, when I noticed a reddish looking dog standing up at the top of a hill, just standing there staring at me. I had a sketchy description of the female dog from Clyde and from a distance this looked like it could be a possibility. It was uncanny how she locked onto me just staring at me almost as if she was luring me toward her. It became obvious to me she was wanting me, no beckoning me to follow her. I believe she knew I was searching for her and she may well have known why. As I got closer, she started to bark at me and retreated a little bit. I could see at that point that this was indeed a recent mother of a sizable litter because she showed all the signs of motherhood. Her nipples were all stretched out from trying to feed the large litter of puppies.

I got relatively close to her when she retreated around the back of a house to which she was luring me all the while. Somehow she slipped back through a hole in the fence in what would later seem like a desperate, last ditch effort on her part, to get help for her and the remainder of the puppies. As I followed her around to the backyard seven more puppies scurried for cover wherever they could find it. They were obviously frightened by the sight of me which made me believe they certainly weren't used to seeing many if any people. They scattered like cockroaches when a light is turned on. All I could see were balls of fuzz and butts diving into or under anything that might provide some refuge from this intruder.

As I surveyed the disaster area, I was confronted with a sight I'm not sure I've ever seen anything like before in my life. I'm not sure I can describe the scene sufficiently enough to explain the knot quickly tightening in my stomach. Looking at the yard and the condition of the rest of the house, it was fairly obvious to me that no one had been around here caring for these puppies for quite some time.

The yard was in absolute shambles! Hell, it looked like a bomb went off in there! The yard was a mud-hole and there was trash strewn from one end to the other. I suddenly realized why the puppy back home was so filthy dirty and flea ridden. As far as I could tell, neither the adult dog nor the puppies had access to any food or water. The only shelter to speak of was a rickety old shed which most of the puppies dove under through a series of holes and trenches they had dug to get under the structure. This was their pitiful existence in terms of shelter from heat, rain, or cold. And at this time of year in Jacksonville, it's a bone chilling damp cold that blows in off the St. John's River. Beyond the cold, there is no telling what eight puppies and their full grown mother had been finding for nourishment for the past several weeks. It was a heartbreaking existence at best and while it tugged tightly at my heart, it made me absolutely sick to my stomach.

I think I stood there, for what seemed an eternity, completely stunned and in total disbelief at the sight before my eyes. If I hadn't known better it would have been easy to imagine myself in a third-world country. There was nothing but bare ground, the clutter of trash and the rickety old shed. It was certainly out of place in this suburban neighborhood of Jacksonville. I suppose I was astounded damn near as much as I was appalled at the conditions these creatures of God were subjected to in eking out their very meager existence.

Noticing all the trash spread across the "lawn", I figured

Christmas Eve 2005

there was no telling when they last had any substantive food to eat. And Lord only knows if they had any source of water to drink. By the look of the backyard, the mother was scavenging food from every trash can within who knows how many miles of the place. As I accounted for the puppies in their attempt to elude my intrusion, I suddenly realized that the puppy back home was definitely the runt of this large litter. It was evident he was the tiniest one in an extremely desperate situation where survival of the fittest was certainly an understatement. At best, he was only half the size of the smallest of the other seven puppies. His chances of surviving the conditions in which he had been thrust in his short lifetime were slim at best.

I had seen all I needed to see. In fact, it was about all I could take. So in less than a good mood, I went around to the front of the house to see if anyone was home. There were boxes piled up on the front porch and the overhead porch light was on but neither my knocking on the door, nor ringing of the doorbell produced anyone from within. I suddenly began to wonder just how long these "pets" had been left alone to fend for themselves. One thing was certain, I would be back looking for the homeowner and I assumed the owner of the dogs. As enraged as I was at that moment, it was probably best for all concerned that no one answered the door that day because there's no telling what the results of that conversation may have been.

I was furious with the irresponsibility of anyone that could allow this dog and her innocent puppies to fend for themselves in such disgusting conditions. But I was convinced of one thing, I wasn't going to stand for it. I would do whatever I needed to in order to extract the remainder of those animals from the awful circumstances in which they were trying to survive.

I went back to the in-law's house and by this time, the puppy seemed to already be the focus of everyone's attention. His first official new bed was a Budweiser box but he quickly moved up to a "Jacksonville Recycle's" bin because he had already figured out how to tip over the cardboard box and have free run of the backyard. So Clyde got one of the recycle bins and put a soft rug for a bed and some extra towels to keep him warm. While my father-in-law likes dogs, I can honestly say in the fourteen years that I'd known him, I've never seen him react this way. There was something different at work here, something special in his reaction to this little guy. It wouldn't be long until it affected us all.

When I got back into the house everyone was anxious to know whether or not I found the mother or owners. Of course, I said I did find what I believed to be the mother but not the owner. I was also quick to explain that this little guy is not going back into that environment if I have anything to say about it. When I finished explaining what I had just witnessed in terms of the living conditions for all of those animals, the vote, if there really was a vote, was unanimous. This puppy escaped a bad situation and deserved a better life and we were going to rally around him. Maybe that's what the mother dog was hoping for when she attracted me to her. Staring at me, from atop the hill, enticing me to follow her. Something deep inside tells me over and over again that she lured me around that house to the backyard in some glimmer of hope of finding a way out for all of them. I began to wonder, "did she abandon him as we originally thought or, did she bring him out onto the streets hoping to provide him a better chance of escaping the sorry conditions in which he was currently living?" Or was it Mother Nature taking its course and weeding out the weak to preserve the stronger puppies. I guess we'll never know but in my gut I have a pretty good idea.

Teresa had already been burning up the telephone lines calling some veterinarians to see about what to feed the little guy, which was good because I was about to embark on a shopping trip to Wal-Mart on Christmas Eve of all things. Bless her heart, Teresa spent the next couple of hours calling every organization in the city we could think of to find some help. In addition to numerous veterinarians' offices she contacted Jacksonville animal rescue, the Police and Sheriff's departments, and SPCA. Of course, on Christmas Eve they were either closed or otherwise too preoccupied to provide much immediate help to our "emergency."

I suppose it is the case in any other town in America, that Wal-Mart on Christmas Eve is an absolute zoo. Jacksonville's brand new superstore was certainly no exception. The first clue was that parking spaces took a minimum of three trips around the enormous parking lot and stalking anyone who gave a remote sign of being ready to leave. The second clue was having finally found a parking space, I headed into the store with my list in hand and there wasn't a single shopping cart to be found. Not one! I thought, "Oh this is going to be fun."

All the insignificant annoyances really didn't matter because I was a man on a mission. I needed to search for all the things it would take to clean the little guy up, get rid of the fleas and get him eating something substantial. I fought my way through the harried crowd to the pet department to pick up some puppy formula. I threw in a puppy flea collar not knowing if we could use it or not because we had no idea just how old the little guy was. We were all thinking he was 4 – 5 weeks at best but we really couldn't be sure.

From the pet department, I fought my way through the hoard of last minute, desperate shoppers to the automotive department in search of some towels or rags that may perform double-duty to either dry the puppy

Christmas Eve 2005

after the upcoming baths or used for bedding. While I had some success there I still headed to the bath supplies section to look over any other possibilities for towels. I found some nice hand towels on sale there for $1.20 apiece and picked up six of them. Two more items and a lot of luck, I could try to get out of this madhouse. On the way to find the Dawn dishwashing liquid, which was recommended by the veterinarian that Teresa talked to for killing the fleas, I found a nice plastic Christmas tub that looked like the old fashioned galvanized aluminum tubs we used growing up for either for washing the dogs or icing down the beer. It would be perfect to give the little guy a thorough and much needed cleansing.

After my uplifting experience at Wal-Mart, I headed back to "rescue central." By the time I got back home, Clyde had gotten the pup all nestled comfortably into his new bed. For the next few days, that recycle bin would become his bed, his comfort zone. He had stacked a myriad of rugs, tee shirts, and other soft rags in the bottom for bedding to rival a four star hotel. He had also hooked up an old desk lamp to shine into the puppy's bed to provide some additional warmth following his impending two baths to rid him of his fleas. The puppy was so wracked out I couldn't bring myself to wake him from such a good sound sleep.

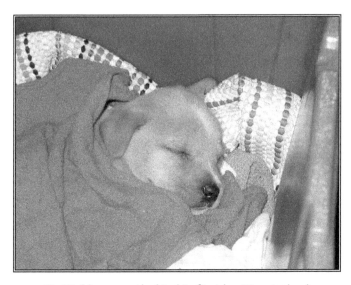

St. Nicklaus nestled in his first legitimate bed.

While the puppy got what was obviously some much needed rest, I suggested the four of us begin a dialogue on possible names for him since he wasn't going anywhere and was now totally our responsibility. Names ranged from Ferber (which was the street on which we found him), to Miracle Whip since his story was quickly becoming some small miracle in and of itself. But being one that believes that a dog's name should be one of meaning I suggested that we call him Saint Nicholas. After all it was Christmas Eve when blessings abound. Little did we know how many blessings he would bestow upon us over the next seven days. The only stipulation was that all of our other dogs over the years have been named for some significant

Christmas Eve 2005

person related to my passion for golf. So, the Nicholas in Saint Nicholas would become Nicklaus after the greatest player to every play the game, Jack Nicklaus. Henceforth, Saint Nicklaus it was. Nicklaus for short and just plain Nick as time would move on.

Unbeknownst to any of us Nicklaus was beginning to cast his magical spell. Suddenly everyone's focus was on his well-being. For the first time in the last ten years of being at the in-laws for Christmas we did not attend the Christmas Eve candlelight service in order to continue the process of caring for little Nicklaus' every need. First on the agenda was a bath to rid him of his fleas.

We setup the bath tub out on the back patio and began transporting buckets of warm water for Nicklaus' first bath. I sure hated to wake the little guy but we had to get those fleas off of him. We found out from one of the veterinarians to put a couple of drops of Dawn dishwashing liquid into the bath water in order to kill the fleas. I woke Nicklaus up from his deep sleep, gave him a chance to get his wits about him, and then took him out to do his business in the grass. I picked the little guy up and proceeded across the patio to the waiting tub of warm water. Slowly I pried his moist little nose off my neck and slowly dipped him into the warm water. He couldn't have been more of a trooper while being baptized for the first time and having the warm soapy water massaged across his entire body. He stood quietly while I lightly scrubbed his little body only looking up at me with those big brown eyes as if to say, "Thanks I can't tell you how good this feels." Low and behold that first scrubbing brought the water to a brown muddy color in short order and was riddled with lots of black specks floating across the top of the water. Much to our pleasant surprise many of the fleas had met their demise. The Dawn detergent had done a great job on combating his flea infestation. Besides that, he sure did smell a whole lot better and that puppy fur of his fluffed up making him as soft as a stuffed toy. Really nice for snuggling!

St. Nicklaus getting comfort from his first mother.

After a thorough soaking and massage fit for a king,

Christmas Eve 2005

I rinsed Nicklaus with clean warm water and then brought all three and a half pounds of him out of the tub and wrapped him in a bath towel. While I dried him the best I could with a couple of towels, Teresa and Clyde were getting a hairdryer ready to help dry the little guy off quickly in an effort to keep him from getting cold. I guess the heat was soothing because he never made a sound or squirmed like it bothered him one bit. We dried his head and ears mostly with a towel and kept the dryer at a distance in an effort to ensure we didn't spin him into a panic or do any damage to his young ears in any way.

By now it was closing in on 4:30 p.m. and we were due at my brother-in-law's house across town for a Christmas Eve social and dinner. The first bath did a good job on the fleas but there were still a great many on Nicklaus even though the bath water was speckled black with the dead ones. We proceeded to repeat the procedure and bathed him for the second time. Again, Nicklaus was cooperative and seemingly grateful for everything we were doing to help him. Looking back on it I guess he really didn't have much of a choice but I believe he understood this was all for his own good. Surely getting those nasty, bloodsucking fleas off his little body had to provide a welcome level of comfort and relief.

As soon as we had him dry from his second luxury

bath, it was time to try to see if we could get him to eat. While I finished drying Nicklaus and let him chase me around the back yard, Teresa whipped up some puppy formula for his first trial run at eating. There wasn't much "trial" about anything to do with food. He jumped in with both front feet, literally, and lapped up that formula like there was no tomorrow. We could tell that this was a very young puppy because when he started to eat the formula you could actually hear him suckling in an attempt to get the milk, like he was used to doing for the past couple to three weeks. That first bowl full of food didn't stand a chance and he polished it off completely and in record time.

St. Nicklaus lapping up one of his first meals.

Isn't it encouraging and refreshing how people rise to

an occasion or reach out to help when someone or in this case, something is in dire need of some TLC. Here it was Christmas Eve, a time filled with so many traditions and annual customs that had become overshadowed, even set aside by something so small yet so hugely important. It was the season for giving and the four of us were giving Nicklaus our all so he may experience a better time, place and enjoy a better life. I remember there was such a sense of purpose for his well-being that each of us was quickly overcome, more accurately, obsessed with providing the little guy with the best chance at life that we may be able to afford him. He filled our hearts with a renewed love of what is important in life and surreal feeling of the spirit that is Christmas. Had we no other gifts to exchange that year we would have still been blessed with one of the greatest Christmas gifts any of us have ever received and perhaps ever will.

With all the excitement of bathing and eating, Nicklaus was more than ready for another nap. That was good because it gave the rest of us an opportunity to get our own showers and change clothes to head out for dinner. Of course since Nicklaus was the first one of us to be cleaned up and ready to step out, he was going to dinner with us. When we were all ready we gathered up all our things we were supposed to take along including the recycle bin and Nicklaus wracked out asleep in his new bed. Much to our surprise, he slept the entire 20-30 minutes it took to get across town and out to Jax beach. Not a peep. Not a whimper. I'm not sure he even turned over, opened an eye, or raised his head during the shuffle through the cross town traffic.

Once we arrived at the oyster roast with Nicklaus in tow and much to the anticipation of the awaiting crowd, I took him out of the recycle bin and onto the front lawn. Of course as he was quickly becoming accustomed to, he did his business as soon as he hit the grass.

While most of the action was taking place outside around the grill to roast the oysters, Nicklaus was content to sleep some more in his new found, warm bed. The nephews, Jonathan and Zachary, were both enamored with the puppy just as the rest of us had become. The remainder of the crowd, young and old alike were all immediately smitten with him. Even though Nicklaus was more than content to sleep the evening away, everyone who saw him couldn't help but pick him up and snuggle with him a little bit. His natural magnetism was affecting everyone he came in contact with.

I've often heard about people with "**it**". You know those people that have that something special that when they walk into a room, a party, a meeting, they instantly attract the attention of everyone else in the room. Well it certainly didn't take long, in fact only a few short hours, to figure out that Nicklaus had whatever "**it**" is. As more people showed up at the oyster roast all of them, each and every one, had to take their turn at holding or cuddling the little fellow. Cousins, in-laws, parents, grandparents, all lined-up to take their turn to shower the charismatic little puppy with some loving before passing him on to the next person in line. If there was any doubt that **"it"** exists, Nicklaus is proof that "it" in fact does.

Nephew Zachary and Nicklaus

Nicklaus slept the entire trip back home as well. Meanwhile I contemplated what a long night I believed I might be in for tonight. I've been through those first nights before with puppies when they realize mother is no longer there for warmth, milk, or general protection. I was certainly not expecting I would be getting much, if any, sleep on this Christmas Eve. But it really didn't matter at that moment. Within a short few hours, Nicklaus was already well worth any effort it took to make sure he was safe, secure, and outwardly content in his new found world. Not that it was nonexistent before but somehow there was a mystical (even magical) growth of oneness, a common goal between the four of us to work toward. There was an unquestionable coming together, a familial bonding if you will, each and every one of us focusing on the care of this precious little present that had serendipitously been thrust upon us. In this season of giving, even though we thought we were providing something to him, it quickly became evident he was filling us with the wonderful feelings that comprise Christmas..... Love, Hope, and Joy.

Clyde taking Nicklaus for a romp in the backyard.

Day Two

Christmas Day 2005

In retrospect, Nicklaus had just reminded me of Christmases past. For as we lay there in bed, me in mine, Nicklaus in his newly found warm confines, my arm hanging over the edge of the bed with my hand lightly touching him as he slept, I began to revisit those fond memories as clear and vivid as I had in a very long time. Christmas' where as a young boy one of our family traditions (at least for the older family members who knew the true meaning of Santa Claus) stayed up all night to celebrate the joys of the season. As we all grew older and no one needed to worry about keeping the "secret" or fumbling through owner's manuals trying to make sure the toys, bicycles, and other presents were assembled with no left over parts, we eventually graduated to being permitted to stay up into the early hours of Christmas morning, if not all night.

The Haas house on Christmas day was a constant ebb-and-flow of people coming and going. That was Christmas tradition spawned by our family consisting of ten children, of which I was the last. My Mother was undoubtedly a Saint because the last one was more trouble than the other nine put together. So much so that she'd tell me that if "I was the first, I'd still be the last." Some of my siblings were already married with children of their own when I was born, meaning it never took much to gather a significant crowd for a party. I revisited those sights, the sounds, the smells of my mother's cooking, and the joy and laughter of the season that filled our home.

In some ways, in that moment, I felt like that young boy again, not being able to sleep, wrought with the excitement of Christmas morning. Laying in bed listening to the tick-tock of that old dual bell alarm clock and wondering how much longer it would be before Santa would come and we'd charge down the stairs in search of our anticipated treasures.

But on this Christmas my greatest gift had already arrived and he was right at the tips of my fingers.

After making it through the night with much less fuss than I could have ever imagined, Nicklaus let me know he was ready to go out or eat again somewhere around 6:30 a.m. In response to his tiniest of whimpers, I rolled out of bed, got dressed and we headed

Christmas Day 2005

out to the backyard. Admittedly, I am not a morning person so the minimal amount of noise or whimper he could make under normal circumstances was not going to wake me from my usual deep sleep. But I was just attuned to the little guy and I think I didn't sleep nearly as much as I thought. When I look back on it, I think I was wide awake and just anticipating that initial whimper that he might make so I could take him outside if need be.

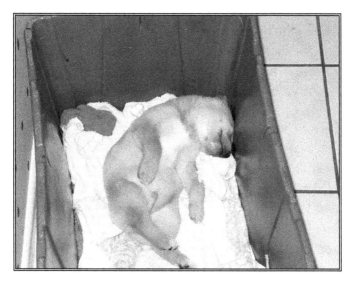

Nicklaus getting one of his many naps.

His habits were quickly becoming commonplace because as soon as he hit the grass, he did his business number one and with a couple of sprints across the backyard chasing me, he took care of number two as well. It was pretty amazing that he would let me know that he had to go, especially considering what his living conditions had been just a little over 24 hours ago where he could go where and when he wanted. But this little guy seemed to grasp the sudden change for the better that his life had taken. At least it sure appeared like he knew!

As planned and discussed the night before, about 9 o'clock Christmas morning I called our good friends the Basher's about Nicklaus. They had just lost one of their dogs right before Thanksgiving and we thought perhaps being the animal lovers that they are they might entertain our plan and be ready to find another dog to fill the void of their recent loss, Bernice.

Bernice was a sweet old Doberman that David and Paula also rescued about eight years earlier having found her as a puppy wondering around the acreage of their large farm. It goes without saying they took that little puppy home and had loved and spoiled her for all those years. I knew how deep a love both David and Paula had for Bernice and I was just a little apprehensive that they might decline our offer to adopt Nicklaus.

David answered the phone and after a few pleasantries of how are you doing and Merry Christmas, I finally got to the real reason for my call.

Christmas Day 2005

I of course started off with all the particulars of how we came across Nicklaus and what I was hoping could be a happy ending for all parties concerned, most importantly, the fate of little Nicklaus. I explained Nicklaus' discovery, abandonment, the baths, his gentle nature and many of his other endearing qualities.

Well Christmas blessings were abounding. David was an extremely gracious listener to the growing legend of Nicklaus and my hope that the Basher's would become a significant part of a story of a lifetime, a story for the ages. While David started out by saying he wasn't sure he was ready for another dog just yet, he did follow-up with an affirmation that, "but we'll certainly look at him." David also went on to say that he'd have to run this by Paula who was unfortunately out of town dealing with an ailing father and by their lone remaining dog, Pee Wee. He wanted to make sure that any new puppy coming on the scene was going to be fully accepted by Pee Wee as well.

You know, the internet when used correctly is just a wonderful tool. We had been snapping pictures of Nicklaus left and right since he'd come into our lives, so sending a couple of "baby" pictures to Paula's email account was no big deal. We sent some of the earliest, most adorable pictures of Nicklaus asleep in his recycle bin bed. So the images of Nicklaus' first night were sent through cyberspace to Paula in Texas for her first visual introduction to Nicklaus. Her immediate reply was something to the effect, "you're not playing fair, he's absolutely adorable, and we'll take him." Again, the agreement was contingent upon Pee Wee agreeing to the deal by accepting a new, lively puppy at her advanced age.

Nicklaus snuggled in for a long nights sleep.

Day Three

Monday 12/26/05

On Monday morning we loaded up the car, Nicklaus and all to begin our four and a half hour journey back home to Aiken. Aiken was going to become Nicklaus' new home one way or the other. Either our friends were going to adopt him or despite Teresa's claim that we couldn't handle three dogs, we would find some way to keep him. Realistically and logistically that would have been a very difficult thing to do with both of us working long hours. But we both knew deep in our hearts, regardless of the difficulty, somehow we would have made it work. The more time we spent with Nicklaus in our arms and laps, the more entrenched he was becoming in our hearts.

Teresa's sister-in-law offered to loan us a portable kennel to transport Nick during the journey to Aiken. It certainly didn't take him any time to get acclimated to his new digs. We weren't quite sure what to expect in terms of his ability to travel. The trip across town on Christmas Eve was not a problem but what about a trip of any length? Our sister-in-law's beagle (and owner of the crate) can't even make it a couple of blocks to the Vets office for checkups without getting car sick. Hopefully, there wasn't a jinx on that crate for Nicklaus and our 4.5 hour trip home.

I don't think we had really gotten out of Jacksonville proper and onto I-95 North before Nicklaus was sound asleep. I suppose most dogs are like children though when it comes to cars, the motion of the vehicle seems to lull them to sleep. We cruised North on I-95 for about 1 ½ hours keeping a constant eye on the little thing looking for any signs that we may need to stop and let him do his business. Although he never made a sound and only woke up once or twice, we thought it best to make a rest stop. As usual, Nick did his routine as soon as we had him out of the car and he hit the grass. This peanut of a puppy was too good to be true. After we all did our business, we saddled-up and got back in the car for the home stretch.

Hardeeville, South Carolina is our usual exit off of I-95 and would be our next stop in about another hour. When we got to Hardeeville we gassed up the car and Teresa took Nicklaus out for a short romp in the grass. It was business as usual as soon as he hit the grass.

Monday 12/26/05

Teresa decided since he was doing so well and sleeping most of the time anyway, she was going to keep him on her lap for the remaining 1 ½ hour drive home. Not to sound like a broken record but once again he gets a gold star. He only woke up occasionally but that was mostly to regroup and snuggle even deeper into Teresa's lap or tuck his head under her arm as he slept.

The ride to Aiken in Teresa's lap.

We were getting home in plenty of time to get to the kennel to pick up our other two boys, Mackenzie and Stewart. Mackenzie, our Welsh Corgi is pedigree all the way, independent, cantankerous, and loving….. on his own terms. Stewart is a rescue dog from the SPCA and is the sweetest, most grateful and loving dog anyone could ever ask for. Unlike Mack, it's as though Stewart knew his fate had we not come along to take him home and he's just appreciative for everything he has or gets. Somehow I already had a suspicion that Nicklaus would have a similar outlook on life in that the "go free card" he'd been dealt for a better life would be exercised to its fullest. I've learned over the years that "rescue" dogs just seem to know when they've been rescued and they show it with loyalty and love to their masters.

When we reached the house we quickly unloaded the car and took Nicklaus still in his crate into the great room. I don't think he even woke up while I carried him into the house. He was sure a tired little thing. So with him settled into his new surroundings, I made a mad dash for the kennel to pick up the boys. Our kennel is operated by our Vet which is a real convenient arrangement not to mention first class care. While I was there I alerted the ladies to the fact that we had rescued this puppy and made an appointment to take him in Tuesday for his initial checkup. Of course they were so excited about Nicklaus and that our friends were considering adopting him. The Bashers use the same Vet service as we do and with all their cadre of animals, they keep the clinic quite busy throughout any given year. The ladies knew just how spoiled and pampered Nicklaus was going to be if they indeed were to adopt him. I retold the past 2 ½ days in detail to them and true to form they couldn't wait to get their eyes and hands on that little bugger.

When I got home from the kennel, it certainly didn't take long for our "boys" (a term given to MacKenzie and Stewart by Martha the kennel manager) to recognize there was something (someone) different in the household. We had discussed whether or not we were going to introduce Nicklaus to Mack and Stewart and decided to keep them apart for two reasons. First, we weren't expecting to keep him. Secondly, he was so tiny we were afraid that the other two could easily hurt him if only by accident.

Nicklaus escaping from his travel crate.

I took Nick for his first walk on the golf course behind our home later that afternoon. I carried all 3 ½ pounds of him out past the back gate. Stewart and Mackenzie were all over me as I walked to the gate. They just had to see what that tiny thing was I was carrying. Overall, they behaved remarkably well. It was much less commotion that I had anticipated by a long shot. Once outside the back gate, I put Nicklaus down and just let him follow me around as he had every time we'd gone outside for the last three days. We walked around the "loop" as it's known at our golf course, holes 16, 17, and 18. Some of the guys in my normal golf group were playing down the 17th hole at the time and all of them scurried over to get a close-up look at Nicklaus.

He was so cute and so small. One of the guys who saw us from a distance said, "I thought you had a pet squirrel following you around." Looking back on it that was a great description because he wasn't much bigger than a squirrel. With each additional person he met, his personality and charisma really began to show through. Everyone wanted to know, "what kind of dog is that?" Followed by, "where did you get him?" Of course all our friends knew about our other two boys at home and they thought we were about to take on a third. I also told everyone of the plan for the Basher's to adopt Nicklaus for a new life on their farm provided everything fell into place correctly.

In fact, David was playing golf that day and got his first look at Nicklaus right there on the golf course. If David wasn't hooked by our previous descriptions and pictures of the little guy, I think seeing him first hand pretty much did him in. If for some reason, this adoption had not happened, for any reason there likely would have been long line of people who would have stepped up and volunteered to take him home.

Nicklaus taking refuge under the Christmas tree.

Nicklaus sure made himself at home in our house and quickly became acclimated to his new surroundings. We had his water bowl in the laundry room and he picked up on that and remembered it immediately. When he was tired, he went in search of his newly acquired crate for a nap. The remainder of the time he pretty much had the run of the house. He spent most of his time running underneath the Christmas tree to satisfy his fascination with the lights and ornaments. While he was cute hiding under there we were cautious (probably over cautious) about him gnawing on the tree lights with those razor sharp teeth. We didn't need anything resembling "Christmas Vacation."

The rest of the time was devoted to running over to the French doors that lead to the sun porch to check out Mackenzie and Stewart. He even had the nerve to peek over the window sash to give out a bark (such as it was) at the boys. Our dogs didn't faze him in the least. Naturally that drove them crazy and they wanted to get to him to check him out. For such a little thing he really didn't exhibit any signs of being scared of anything. Time and time again he'd go to those French doors and stand there nose-to-nose with the boys on the other side without anything between them other than the pane of glass. He'd go wander off into other rooms of the house alone just to do some exploring. At one point he discovered the large mirror we have in our living room and came face-to-face with himself. It was classic but I'm not sure he really knew what to make of what he was looking at. He was certainly fascinated by what he saw but he showed no fear.

Nicklaus staring himself down in the living room mirror.

The fact of the matter was that we had a concern that Mack or Stewart might harm the puppy, whether intentionally or not, but at this point we were also unsure of Nicklaus' medical condition. The last thing we wanted to do was to introduce any disease to our two healthy dogs. So we were diligent about keeping them separated at least until we could get him to our veterinarian for a good checkup. Considering our plans to give him up, we didn't want the three of them to get too accustomed to each other either. So, we just continued to maintain a deliberate distance between them.

Those first few days, the majority of rest periods that

Nicklaus got were in the lap of either Teresa or myself. For as much as he loved to be close to or held by someone, I must admit we couldn't keep our hands off of him either. Nicklaus would sleep in our laps for an hour or two at a time. About the only thing he'd wake up for was his instinctual call of nature. He looked so content, it made both of us envious for an opportunity to ever sleep that soundly.

Snuggle time again.

Day Four

Tuesday, December 27

Teresa and I were scheduled to return to work on Tuesday from the Christmas break but there was no way we could leave the puppy alone all day or with the boys. Plus we needed to get him to the Vet for a good sound checkup. So I called my office and took another day off from work. It wasn't going to be difficult spending another whole day with the little charmer anyway. We realized too, that we would need to take him to "daycare" on Wednesday and Thursday as well so we made arrangements with Martha and Myrna, the kennel staff, to bring him in early morning and pick him up after work. Not surprisingly, they were gracious in agreeing to help however they could. It wouldn't be long until Nicklaus would be casting his spell over them as well. I believe he had already laid that seed.

I scheduled an appointment with our animal clinic

for 10:00 am Tuesday morning to have Nicklaus get a thorough once over. At a mere three-and-a half pounds, there was no telling what he was managing to live on under the miserable conditions in which he was surviving or what contagious diseases he may have been subjected to in his relative short time on this earth.

When I checked in at the front desk, I had all 3 ½ pounds of fluff nestled in the crook of my arm which was becoming a common place for him to cuddle. I think it gave Nick a feeling of contentment and safety but it was as equally satisfying for me as well. I think since we called in advance to schedule the appointment and explained the circumstances of Nick's rescue, there was great anticipation in the air to get a look at the puppy. It didn't take long for the whole office to be buzzing with the excitement of Nicklaus' arrival. The same common themes continued to be tossed about as though scripted, "oh he's so cute," "how adorable", "what kind of dog is he?" Once again, his charisma was hard at work and overwhelming everyone around him. You could literally see it take a firm hold on everyone!

By the time we got into the exam room, we were greeted by not one but two of the clinics Doctors waiting on Nicklaus to give him the "Full Monty" of health exams. As the doctors were beginning the examination,

Tuesday, December 27

the door of the exam room opened and David walked through the door. When we talked the day before I told him about the vet and Nicklaus' exam so he dropped by to see how things were going.

A common position for Nicklaus from day one.

Nicklaus was as good as gold through all the usual poking, prodding and even the shots. He received the full battery of tests, shots (or as many as they thought such a little guy could handle at this point), but the final diagnosis was that he was a healthy puppy and just needed to eat, eat, and eat some more. The other directive was to let Nicklaus start eating some small kibbles puppy food. That news was particularly to Nicklaus' liking!

Nicklaus' first bowl of kibbles.

With a full complement of razor sharp teeth, it certainly made sense that he could chew up the kibbles but we just weren't sure whether his young digestive tract was up for the challenge of hard food. Boy we're we about to find out how wrong that line of thinking was.

We were elated that the initial checkup went well and we had a healthy, happy little thing on our hands and hearts. As we left the doctor's office, David and I discussed getting Nicklaus together with Pee Wee, the second to last hurdle for Nicklaus' adoption by the Bashers. The last was Paula's approval when she got back in town from her trip. That wasn't really of concern because I was sure Nicklaus would win her over just like every other human being he'd come in contact with over the past 48 hours. I believe she was hooked on the pictures alone, so I was confident when she saw Nicklaus in person, she'd melt and it would be a done deal.

Pee Wee and Nicklaus getting acquainted.

I told David that I had made arrangements with the kennel staff to bring Nicklaus in for day care beginning Wednesday until Friday, so he could bring Pee Wee by the kennel for a visit and test run of the 2 dogs. So bright and early Wednesday morning Pee Wee and Nicklaus got together in the grassy run of the kennel and the meeting went without incident. There was a great deal of sniffing of one another going on, mainly on Pee Wee's part I guess trying to figure out who this little guy belonged to. At thirteen and a half years old I'm sure Pee Wee was wondering why he had to be checking out this little live wire of energy. She was probably thinking, "Oh I sure hope this isn't coming home to our house."

Day Five

Wednesday, December 28

Two of my sisters and corresponding brothers-in-law from Pennsylvania our house for a quick on their way to Hilton Head for a golf vacation for a quick visit. They are four card game playing aficionados' and of course we played a number of games into the early hours of the morning during their two day visit. The real reason I mention this is that during all those hours of playing a game or just visiting, someone had Nicklaus in their lap. Of course the Haas family grew up with a variety of pets and the whole family is animal lovers so it didn't take long for all four of the Bozzelli's to become enchanted by Nicklaus' mystic.

Interestingly enough, my sister Donna has had allergies to certain animals (or at least to their fur) for the majority of her life. In true Haas family fashion, she did have dogs in their family over the years, but they were always the variety that had short hair versus fur like the Schnauzer or Airedale breeds. Those breeds apparently did not have an effect on her in terms of allergic reaction. I found it fascinating that first and foremost she never gave a fleeting thought to potential allergic reactions when it came to holding or snuggling with Nicklaus. Again, his magic seemed to be at work as though it were an elixir. She held Nicklaus for the major portion of the time that we were playing various card games. And then she shuffled him off to the recliner where he was content to lay in her lap for some more prolonged snuggling.

My sister Donna and Nicklaus feeling right at home.

Wednesday, December 28

What quickly became a recurring theme was becoming commonplace with everyone that met little Nick. "I don't know how in the world you're going to be able to give that little guy up for adoption?" I recall those words first coming from my sisters after their short encounter with him but those words would be spoken again and again by a large percentage of the people blessed with the opportunity to cross his path. In fact, I recall hearing that comment made a couple of times in Jacksonville and it would become a recurring theme going forward.

As hard as it was to say, our standard answer was that we knew it was going to be difficult, but we also knew it was going to be the right thing to do. It wouldn't be fair to the puppy at his age to be left alone all day while we were at work. After all, that's one of the reasons we rescued Stewart from the SPCA. So he could keep Mackenzie company or vice-versa while we gone during the day. The second reason was that Teresa and I both had a good idea that when this puppy was full grown he was going to need a lot of room to exercise. His anticipated home was going to offer exactly that and more. So while we recognized it was going to be tough to let him go, it was something we realized we had to do.

As I took Nicklaus for walks around the golf course, it became more and more difficult to fathom how this little guy's mother managed to get him to follow her for blocks and blocks with those stubby little legs. When I'd walk him around the golf course, it was all he could do to keep up for 25-30 yards at a time. While he followed me wherever I'd go, it took extraordinary effort on his part to keep pace. If I got too far out in front he'd just plop down and sit there. Of course, I'd back track and usually he was rested and he'd pop up and be ready to continue the journey.

We were getting into a routine of walking the "loop" at Palmetto Golf Course. We'd head out our back door, down the seventeenth fairway, around the clubhouse and back home again. A walk around those 810 yards would normally take about ten minutes but with those sawed-off little legs carrying his body we were averaging about thirty minutes from start to finish. That's not to be taken as a complaint by any stretch, but rather to stress my earlier point about how in the world he managed to tag along with his mother for as long as he did. His personality was certainly taking form and it was one of doing what he could to please us, whatever the cost.

Watching him ramble about on the golf course or in the front yard, I couldn't help but wonder about the fate of the other seven puppies from the litter. We found out a few days later that the SPCA did indeed pay a visit to that disaster area the remaining puppies were existing in and were all rescued. My father-in-law went by that house the following week to check on them and was certain they had all been picked-up by animal control personnel. Watching Nicklaus romping through the grass, that was every bit as high as his legs were long, I could only hope for their sake that all of those puppies found a similar fate. If they were even half as cute, loveable, and cuddly as Nicklaus, surely they all went onto similar good fortune and loving surroundings.

Day Six

Thursday, December 29

Day six started just like the previous five mornings had, with an unbridled anticipation of seeing Nicklaus' adorable face and fuzzy little body. Taking him out for his morning jaunt around the front yard, letting him stretch those short little legs and use all his faculties. It was still amazing to me just how quickly he caught on to the routine and how smart this little guy really was.

We were facing the reality that we were mere hours away from giving up this little bundle of joy and somehow the anxiety and certainty was beginning to set in. While we continued to struggle with our decision, even our ultimate decision to let go of Nick and actually give him up for adoption, our parental instincts kicked in compelling us to compose a 'set of instructions" to the soon to be new parents.

Thursday, December 29

Romping in the front yard with a water bottle nearly as big as he was and weighed just about as much.

A set of instructions for God's sake, to the very people we trusted enough to call and convince that this puppy was something they truly wanted, truly needed. I remember thinking "advice on how to care for this little guy to two individuals who are animal lovers that could match all others." But yet, in our admittedly crazed state, it had to be done. We were compelled to let them know as much as we could about Nicklaus and all we had learned about him over the past six days. How he loved to be held, touched, sleep, what he was eating, when and how we took him outside to do his business. Anything and everything we could think of that would make their adoption and Nick's adaptation to his new home and family easier for him as well. Here's a copy of the text from that letter:

David and Paula,

Nicklaus has had very few mishaps in terms of accidents in the crate or in the house. He is almost house broken as long as you take him outside onto the grass as soon as he comes out of his crate. He may pee two or three times in a row and then maybe poop. He has been very good about letting you know when he has to do something. If he starts whining you probably want to take him outside to do his business. The first couple of nights he woke up needing to go outside in the early morning (2:30 A.M., 4:00 A.M.) but last night (12/30) he slept straight through until almost 5:45 A.M. without doing anything in the crate. So his stamina is increasing. <u>He's a great traveler too</u>.

He loves to be held and will curl up in your arms and fall asleep in an instant. I've been holding him in my lap, and he's usually asleep, for an hour or two before bed. I've taken him out right before bedtime and then put him in his crate and he has just nodded right off to sleep. He has whined once or twice when I put him into the crate but I just stick my finger through the crate door to pet him or let him suckle my finger and he'd go right to sleep.

I've been putting an alarm clock in his crate which helps with his sleeping. I think it's like his mother's or sibling's heartbeat, but whatever it is, he loves it. He's been sleeping with his head or body right on top of the clock. The other thing I've done which seems to help is to pile my clothes just outside his crate door where he can see and smell them. That seems to have comforted him as well to help him fall asleep quickly.

Because he's so small, I have not put any water container inside the crate. Some crates come with plastic cups to latch onto the crate door. I don't like those, especially given his size. I had the cup on the door the other day and Nicklaus was resting his head on it to sleep. I was afraid the little fellow could drown if he fell asleep so that was history and not in use.

Keep in mind he is teething and will chew on anything he can get those razor sharp teeth into. So you need to watch out for his fascination within electrical cords, speaker wires, your hands, etc. He's also a lot faster than you may think and you have to be careful when he's running loose in the yard or house not to step on him. There have been a number of times when I couldn't find him and he was right under or between my feet and I never saw how he got there. He's quick!

We've been feeding Nicklaus about ½ cup of puppy chow three times a day. You can experiment with other kibbles if you want, but I'd highly recommend staying away from the Avoderm puppy products. The Vets continue to tout it even after explaining his reaction to it but I'd stay clear of it. David and I discussed Nicklaus' reaction to that food. He was so hyper (actually uncontrollable) it was scary. Especially for a puppy that otherwise is so laid back and attentive.

Teresa and I are so happy that Paula and you decided to adopt Nicklaus although we are very heavy hearted to see him go. We think you're getting a very special dog based upon how much we've both fallen in love with him in a matter of seven days. We wracked our brains since we've been home as to how we might be able to keep him since he has absolutely stolen or hearts, but we know it's just not realistic for us to do so. So we're proud to have played a part in saving him and bringing you guys together for what we know will be a long, happy and healthy life and he'll get all the love, care and nurturing, he so rightly deserves.

Dale & Teresa

St. Nicklaus and Teresa.

As I lay there in bed in the early morning hours, my arm draped over the side of the bed so my hand could reach and touch Nicklaus while he slept, I found myself wondering, thinking, about this obsession, this burning desire to reach out to help these creatures. This was certainly not the first rescue I've performed in my life although I wasn't prepared for just how difficult the days ahead would be for us to "let go" in this case.

Knowing the hours before giving Nicklaus up to his new parents were rapidly upon us, I flashed back to a few years earlier when I rescued another puppy from certain peril, then another, and another all in rapid succession. These were not dreams since I was wide awake and I relived each one in specific detail as though it had happened only yesterday. The following are just a few examples of some of the other dogs that I've crossed paths with over the years. If as the old saying goes, "everything happens for a reason" is true, and I'm a firm believer it is, then I was in the right place at the right time when it comes to rescuing these puppies.

"In Quite a Pickle"

It was a rainy afternoon as I was driving home from work. I decided to take the back way home for a nice leisurely drive to relax, unwind and try to leave the happenings of the day at the office. This was a rural county road with not too many houses rather more farms with their fields planted in either, corn, soybeans, cotton, or other southern crops, or plowed under laying fallow for a few months. As I drove along, I noticed the back end of a black dog wondering strangely across the rows of furrows of a freshly plowed field. At first glance, I couldn't make out if he was chasing something or digging after some burrowing animal. All I could really make out from a distance was that his butt was sticking up in the air and he was obviously serious about whatever it was he was doing.

I slowed down the car to get a better look at what he was up to and suddenly realized he wasn't digging, eating, or chasing anything. He was actually struggling quite unsuccessfully to pry his head out of a plastic pickle jar. God only knows where he may have located a pickle jar out here in the middle of nowhere but that jar was securely fastened around his head and neck and he was struggling mightily to pry himself loose from his plastic captor.

Bless his heart, there's no telling how long that jar around had been his head and neck. He was wondering around in the middle of the field, the nearest little farm house probably 200 yards away with no one in sight that might help him escape from this predicament he had gotten himself into. I parked the car and ran across the field to where he was struggling to free himself. I was immediately concerned about how long he had been this way and whether he was getting enough air to keep from suffocating.

Since I was on my way home from work I was in a coat and tie since "casual dress" was not yet in vogue, here I was trudging across this freshly plowed, muddy field to get to this helpless dog. It was probably a good forty to fifty yards across the field from where I had parked the car.

When I finally reached him, I began talking to him in as calm a voice as I could so as to not panic him anymore than his current state of anxiety. I just kept talking the closer I got until he could heard my voice. When he finally heard my voice, he stopped clawing and scratching at the rim of the pickle jar and turned toward my voice. Well if it wasn't for the fact that I knew we had a serious situation here, I could have fallen down laughing at the sight of this dog with this plastic pickle jar helmet plastered on his head. I can only imagine how he felt looking through the murky, whitish plastic at this human calling out to him or wondering if I was going help or harm him in his totally defenseless state.

I kept talking to him to keep him calm while I tried to secure him and pry my fingers between the rim of the jar and his neck. I couldn't believe how tight this thing was. I was wondering if he was getting any air at all. How am I going to get this thing off I thought. Am I going to have to try to cut it off somehow? One other consideration I hadn't even thought about until much later was, is he mad as hell and going to take my hand off when and if I did get him free of this plastic noose.

I tried to straddle him so I could steady him as I stuck my fingers in between the rim of the jar and to my surprise there was a fair amount of room. It didn't seem as tight around the dog's neck as I had imagined, but it was securely fixed over the backside of the dogs ears

Thursday, December 29

which is most likely what kept him from freeing himself despite the all-out effort he gave in trying to scratch or claw himself free. It quickly became evident that I was not going to be able to pry the jar free from this position so I went around front and grabbed the jar at the bottom with both hands, all the while still talking to the puppy trying to reassure him I was a friend trying to help. I got as strong a grip as I could with both hands on the bottom of the jar and gave it one quick jerk. The jar popped off of that black lab's head sending me a couple of feet backward upon its final release. I somehow managed to maintain my balance and keep from falling on my butt and into the muddy field beneath my feet. When I looked down at the black lab, I saw the most grateful face I may have ever caught a glimpse of in my entire life.

What happened next was pretty much a blur for the next thing I knew I was being lashed with the coldest, wettest tongue that even the chilly rain hitting my face couldn't match. There was a sudden explosion of joy and thankfulness by the puppy for his new found freedom. There were muddy paws flying at me from every direction. I wasn't sure if I had freed an octopus or a dog. It sure seemed like more legs and paws whirling around me than the standard four.

There I stood, in the rain a muddy mess. My shoes, pants, white shirt, and tie all covered with mud splattered paw prints. I couldn't help but chuckle when I looked down at my white shirt that I looked like some kindergarten paint project. But I remember feeling so full of life at that moment that a little mess was well worth the joy I was able to impart on another living creature. I took the pickle jar with me and told the lab to "go home", assuming he belonged at the farmhouse in the distance. After a great deal of coaxing I finally got him to realize that he was not going home with me and managed to get him to stay while I made my way back to the car. He just sat there staring at me until I had gotten in the car and began to drive off. Then he turned and headed toward the farmhouse as we both went our separate ways but truly thankful for our paths having crossed.

In all the days of driving along that same road going to and from work over the next few years, I never saw that black lab again. Sometimes I'd just chuckle to myself and think, "maybe, I just can't recognize him without his pickle jar."

"Midnight"

It was a beautiful July morning in South Carolina, the kind that makes you want to tee off early in order to beat the oppressive heat you know will build up by mid-afternoon. Teresa and I teed off at 8:15 am settling into a nice pocket behind some other foursomes already ahead of us on the course. By the time we reached the third hole, the sun was beginning to beat down relentlessly. Out of nowhere a black dog appeared standing there looking at the two of us. We'd later realize he had been hiding under a large bush seeking some refuge from the impending blast of heat. He was black from head to toe, the only thing white on him was the undersides of his ears that flopped up and down as he pranced around. I could only imagine that all that black fur he was sporting had to be extremely hot when exposed to the blistering sun.

He was a handsome dog but sure was skittish and very cautious about getting too close to us. We had no idea how long he might have been out roaming the golf course, how far he might have come, or whether he had anything to eat or drink in the recent past. We had a pack of Lance crackers in our golf bag which we carried for a snack later in the round, so we pulled those out and tried to coax him closer in order to gain some trust. It was obvious from his skittishness that he had no intention of getting too close or taking any chances that we might harm him in some way. He was trusting of no one. As I tore the cellophane wrapper off the crackers, it didn't take long to get his undivided attention. I broke up the first cracker and tried to lure him to come closer and retrieve the treat. The best I could do was to toss it to him some five feet away. Even the motion of tossing the cracker in his direction sent him reeling in retreat. With each successive cracker however, he became a bit more trusting and even began to follow us as we played the next few holes. The fourth tee box has a water cooler, so we took a Styrofoam cup from our golf cart and put some water in it and set it down so he could get a cool drink of water. He drank every drop but not without a watchful eye to make certain we didn't make any unsuspected moves. I actually saw another cup on the ground where one of the groups in front of us must have had the same idea and gave him a drink of water as well. We would come to discover cups around the front-nine of the course where other golfers had obviously left him water to drink as well. As we continued on, he followed us for a few more hole, or darted ahead to find a shady spot from which he could watch our progress and I assume hoping to cop another morsel of food. After about the sixth hole, he suddenly vanished. We assumed he was back-tracking his route to find the next group of golfers who might be willing to provide something else to eat.

The fourteenth tee box is adjacent to the third fairway and after not seeing him for the past eight holes, suddenly there he was again. He was ghostly for sure, now you see me, now you don't. If he had been a white dog I'd already nicknamed him Casper after the loveable cartoon character. But he was black as coal and it seemed more likely that "midnight" might be a more suitable name. Maybe his black coat allowed him to

Thursday, December 29

dart in and out of the deep shadows unnoticed. I'm not sure, but he could vanish and reappear like magic. As we finished up the fourteenth hole, we noticed him heading across the first fairway and up the cart path toward the clubhouse. A group on the first tee saw him coming and put down yet another cup of water for him to drink. I think he was beginning to feel at home at our private club although that was the last we saw of him as we played our last four holes.

We finished up and headed home for lunch and for Teresa to begin packing for her business trip to Washington, DC on Monday. She planned on leaving the house around 3:30pm in order to catch her 5:30pm flight. As a result, I had already planned to play some more golf, most likely another eighteen holes, which is exactly what I did. It had been nearly four hours now since we had last seen "midnight" so I just figured he found his way out the front gate of the club and made his way home. I was sure and mentioned to Teresa earlier that I thought I had seen that dog somewhere before. I was beginning to believe he lived across the street from the golf club. To be honest, I really expected that he had found his way out of the club and hopefully had found his way home, safe and sound. Consequently, the last thing I expected was to drive up to play my second shot on the third hole, the same place we had seen him earlier in the morning and after stopping the cart and grabbing a club, there he stood. He had sneaked up behind me and had magically reappeared yet again.

While he seemed to be a bit more approachable, he was still living within a cautions bubble of space between himself and me. I played my second shot to the green and drove off. He quickly followed me. When I parked the cart I went over to the water cooler and filled up the cup that we had left for him earlier in the morning with more water. I began rummaging through my golf bag to see what other treats I might have in there that I could share with him again. Fortunately I found a Rice Krispy treat bar and the sound of the cellophane certainly perked up his floppy ears. I tried to get him to come close enough to take a piece of the treat from my hand.

He was still taking no chances and I had to toss it to him. I tossed the next one a little closer to me and he moved in and gobbled it up but not without keeping a close eye on my every move. I mean one twitch of my other hand and he jumped back like his legs were made of springs. Again, another piece and I tossed it to him but closer to me again. Since I had not moved any closer to him or into his space, I finally put the next piece out at arms-length and he took it out of my hand. Another piece, and again he took it gently from my fingertips. I fed him the remainder of the treat from my hand and as quickly as he finished off the entire bar,

Thursday, December 29

he backed away to a safe distance. With nothing left in my bag of treats to feed him, I went back to playing some more golf. He followed me for the next four holes staying within distance where I could talk to him in comforting tones or put down another cup of water for him to drink. But he wasn't getting overly trusting of me yet. I didn't give up hope though because when he disappeared again and headed in the direction of another group coming along, I could tell he was no more trusting of any of them than he was of me. I didn't see him again for nearly six more holes. In fact, I heard him before I saw him this time.

I was now on hole number twelve when his howls echoed throughout the pines of the golf course. He was lying on the tee box of the sixth hole about two hundred and fifty yards from the twelfth green howling incessantly. I teed off of the thirteenth hole and he stayed put on the sixth tee just watching me as I approached. Again, I retrieved some snacks out of my golf bag and tried to lure him close to feed him. He came by the golf cart and I threw him a piece of cracker. He cautiously accepted the treat but only from a few feet that could allow him to feel safe. As I walked off the thirteenth green, he was still lingering around in hope of getting more to eat and I, was of course, happy to oblige. Unfortunately it didn't take long for him to devour the whole pack of crackers. As I played off the fourteenth tee I suddenly realized he was nowhere to be found. I had no idea where he disappeared too. Once again he had done a Houdini act essentially vanishing right before my eyes.

I finished the round and saw no further sign of Midnight so I walked home to take my "boys" for a walk, take a shower and have some dinner. Since it was summer and daylight savings time was in full swing I finished dinner and decided to walk back over to the clubhouse to see if he might still be hanging around. Just in case I might encounter him again I filled a sandwich bag with some kibbles knowing he would welcome more food.

As I walked across the practice green, a friend of mine was practicing his chipping and putting and I asked him if he had by any chance seen a black dog hanging around. Sure enough he said he was just there a few minutes ago. So I set out to the front side of the clubhouse to see if I could locate him again. Just as the rest of the day, he reappeared again literally out of thin air. The only place I could figure he came from was out of one of the treacherously deep bunkers that line the eighteenth fairway and the eighteenth green. But wherever he came from, there he was again.

As I called to him and tried to get him to come closer, I reached into my pocket and revealed the baggie full of food. At first he was still as leery of me as he was earlier in the day. As I reached into the baggie, the rustling of the plastic or perhaps the smell of the kibbles certainly gained his undivided attention. I sat on the brick steps of the clubhouse and flipped a couple of kibbles onto to the brick patio three or four feet away to satisfy his comfort level and once again regain his trust. I kept tossing kibbles but decreasing the distance between him and myself, slowly luring him closer and closer.

It took nearly 45 minutes and the majority of the bag of food but I finally gained enough trust in Midnight to have him eating out of my hand again. With each subsequent handful of kibbles, he gobbled them down right out of my hand until finally he had eaten the entire bag. It was at this point, he finally allowed me into his space to actually pet him. We sat there together, me petting him and him becoming more comfortable and trusting of me.

I wasn't sure what to do at that point since I didn't think I could put him in the back yard with my two dogs not knowing how they or he would react. I certainly didn't want to frighten him any further or heaven forbid have them get into any kind of scuffle. I thought perhaps having been fed and cared for that perhaps he would hang around the clubhouse and in the morning we might be able to somehow locate his owners. I got up and started to walk toward the house with Midnight following close behind shadowing my every move all the way to the walkway into the gate of my backyard.

It was getting well past dusk now and I walked through the gate and locked it behind me. As I got closer to the back door of the house, I looked over my shoulder and there was Midnight standing up, both front paws on the top of the gate peering into the backyard begging to come in. It was absolutely heartbreaking, but I just wasn't trusting of Mackenzie and Stewart to be overly sociable to the newcomer. The dilemma was I didn't think I could bring him into the fenced-in yard to ensure he'd hang around. I also wasn't sure if I left him outside the fence that he would stay, so I figured the next best thing would be to put down a bowl of water and a plate with more kibbles. That seemed like it was going to be a workable solution since he was lapping up both the food and water as if he hadn't eaten all day. I was pretty sure since he knew there was food to be had just past that fence that he might camp out there until morning, so I retreated to the house.

About ten thirty in the evening I took the boys for their last walk of the night before bedtime. As we went out the back gate, the food I'd left on the plate was all gone and so was Midnight. The boys and I took our usual route up the seventeenth fairway about 200 yards and still no sign of him. We went into a wooded area between holes 16 and 17 and suddenly there he stood right next to the three of us. Mackenzie began to growl aggressively and Stewart just wanted to play. Still I wasn't comfortable with letting him in the yard

Thursday, December 29

with the boys for the night. Again, I took him a few more kibbles and managed to pet him goodnight hoping he'd still be there by sun up, I headed to the house and onto bed.

According to the clock radio on the nightstand, it was 1:00 am when I heard Midnight howling like he had earlier in the day. At least I knew he was still out there close by. Now if he'll only stay put until morning, maybe I can find out who was missing him.

I didn't know that I wouldn't need the alarm clock in the morning, but at 5:00 am, the howling began again in earnest. I was overcome with relief knowing that he was still there and maybe I could help him get home. Teresa and I had already discussed getting in touch with our vet's office if Midnight was still around in the morning. They might be able to locate his owner. That same approach had be successful in the past with a Standard Poodle we rescued a few years ago and we were hopeful we could turn this into another happy ending as well.

After hearing his searing howl, I jumped from bed and jumped into my clothes, rounded up the boys and headed out the back gate. The boys were getting their usual morning walk but I was on another mission. This would be one final attempt to somehow get Midnight to trust me enough to get a leash around his neck and eventually into the car for a ride to our Vet. I didn't take more than a few steps through the back gate when BOOM there he was staring us all in the face. Remarkably and to my greatest surprise neither Mack nor Stewart did any aggressive move toward the newcomer. There was a bit of sniffing and posturing but not a single growl or threatening move by anyone. So I took the boys on their morning stroll like any other day and Midnight tagged along almost like he'd done this with the three of us many times before. We walked around the loop and back to the house, in lockstep like one big happy family. Since things were going so well, I decided to let Midnight into the back yard trusting that all would continue to go well. Amazingly, everything went fine and all three dogs behaved as though they were family.

I had my cell phone with me already so I sent a text to our Vet and I don't think I had even gotten into the shower when he called me back. Charlie Timmerman has been our Vet for many years and is the most caring, understanding, accommodating individual I have ever met in that profession, perhaps in any profession. He's a blessing to the animals he cares for as well as each and every pet owner who entrusts him to care for their four-legged family members. He's one of those select few people in the world who are lucky enough to be deeply engrossed in a love affair with their job.

As expected Charlie said, absolutely Dale bring him by

Thursday, December 29

and we'll see if we can locate his owners. This was not the first time we've made a similar request to Charlie and it's always the same answer. Basically whatever he can do in the best interest of the animal he will do, just like the consummate professional he has always been. My challenge now became getting Midnight on a leash and into the car to transport to Charlie's office.

I put another handful of kibbles into my pants pocket in anticipation of performing a great deal more bribery in order to get a leash over his head. I had to practically start from scratch to get him to come close enough to eat the kibbles out of my hand. But it didn't take long at all compared to yesterday's ordeal.

I kept petting Midnight and feeding him kibble after kibble, all the while trying to work the choker chain on the leash over my left hand which already contained some kibbles. I figured if he began to eat some out of that hand, I could slowly slide the chain over his snout, head and onto his neck. Sure enough it worked. I managed to get him to eat out of the left hand and slide the collar carefully onto him, just like I visualized.

I wasn't expecting what happened next however. He began to jump and buck like a rodeo bull. I was scared he might hurt himself and I calmly talked to him, petting him some more until he finally settled down. Once he realized I wasn't going to harm him, he lunged back toward me and sat as tight against my leg as he could get. He was literally pasted against my thigh to the point where I could hardly move my leg. In fact, when I started to take a step to lead him to the car he almost tripped me once, twice, three times while trying to take any step forward.

I suppose if anyone had seen us trying to move or had a video of it, you'd have to laugh hysterically at my feeble attempts at the simple act of walking. Me, trying to take a step and he with his body plastered against my leg like a NFL linebacker. But through it all, we finally made it through the backyard, out the gate in the fence (a tight squeeze for the both of us) and to my car in the driveway.

Opening the car door, I cautiously lifted him into the back seat. I say cautiously because he had a full set of beautiful, pearl white teeth that I really didn't want any part of being attached to my body. I'm relieved to report that all went well and I managed to get him into the back seat where he sat comfortably all the way to the Vets office. He sat in the car like a trooper, just looking around at the surroundings and sizing me up as though trying to figure out where we were going. But still he seemed relaxed, giving me the impression perhaps he's been through this routine before.

As we reached the Vets office and I parked the car, he suddenly looked a great deal less comfortable with the situation. I slowly exited the driver's side door, and closed it behind me. Even more cautiously, I opened up the back door keeping my body blocking any option for him to make a mad dash past me. I made sure I had a good grip on the leash before lifting him up and onto the ground. I was glad I had anticipated something like that because as soon as his feet hit the ground, he tried to make a run for it. Thank God for choker chains because without it, I'm convinced that with his tugging and pulling he may have actually slipped out of a conventional collar and been off and running free again, and in all likelihood having little chance of regaining his trust again.

I managed to calm him down and even though he was again becoming skittish over the walk into the lobby area, he his anxiety level was obviously increasing. Between the staff assistant, Christina and me petting and talking to Midnight, we finally got him comforted, under control, and back into a trusting mood. While the two of us continued with the comforting, Charlie and his "Angels" began to check him out and scanned him for a microchip.

Knowing he was in good safe hands and I needing to get to work, I left him in anticipation of him being returned to his rightful home. But not before again telling Charlie as I have numerous times before, "If you don't find the owner, we will keep him (even though we really didn't want to have three dogs). He was too beautiful, too healthy and too sweet to send to the SPCA only to hope that he'd find a good home. Especially after he finally had someone he could or did trust enough to let them let pet him. Thankfully he wasn't threatened by all these strangers and all the things he was being subjected to.

I wasn't far from the office when my cell phone rang. Christina gave me the great news that he in fact had a microchip and they were able to locate his owners. "Midnight's" real name was "Polo" and his owners said he had escaped through a gate that was mistakenly left open. He had been missing and on the loose for the past seven days. I never found out exactly where his home was but the owner, upon finding out where he had been found, was astonished at just how far Polo's sojourn had taken him.

I believe it's events like these in our lives that bring about one's love and desire to care for those less fortunate whether it be caring for an animal or family, friends, neighbors, or even strangers. I'm also convinced that with each such event, where you are able to help someone or something in need, your desire to continue to provide such assistance grows deeper and stronger.

It strikes me after all these years that perhaps all those early television shows and movies of the 1950's and beyond had a profound effect on the baby boomer generation. With the possible exception of "Old Yeller" and regardless of how many flips and flops the story line may have taken, or how desperate the primary characters found themselves in, ninety-percent ended on a happy note.

I love happy endings. Wouldn't you agree?

Day Seven

Friday, December 30

One last jaunt in the front yard.

The anticipation of taking Nicklaus and dropping him off at his new home reminded me of my childhood when our dog Patch had a litter of 7-8 puppies. At the time I was about 5 years old and if I was even in school yet, it was only kindergarten. Consequently, I spent hour upon hour playing with all of those puppies in our basement and backyard. Watching them run, play, fight, and bite ears (mine included). Spending so much time with something so cute makes it difficult not to become attached to them. I remember becoming overly fond of one in particular which I named "Nip." I'm not sure where that name came from (perhaps it was from the RCA mascot "Nipper"), but it stuck. She and I became best buddies in a relatively short amount of time before the entire litter would be going to their new homes. Perhaps this was a precursor to the feelings I was currently having about Nicklaus.

I can clearly recall that day when all those puppies were to be given away to new homes, new masters, and totally gone from our lives. Nip was going to be particularly difficult with which to part company. I watched and cried as all those fluff balls were herded up and put into a cardboard box for transport by their new owner. I know I cried all the way up the cellar steps, through the house and out to the front porch trying like crazy to be able to keep Nip. Finally, I guess I was so pitiful and I wore my Mother down so much that she stopped the man, reached down into the box and retrieved Nip from the remainder of the litter and handed her to me. We had that dog, what I considered to be my first one, for about 11 or 12 years.

The rush of those past but familiar emotions were certainly coming back to me loud and clear that morning when we knew we would be giving Nicklaus up to his new home and parents. But even with that flood of emotions, there were many things that made the idea somewhat easier.

First and foremost we knew that David and Paula would be over-the-top parents and companions for the little guy, just as they have been over the years with all of their other pets and animals. Secondly, and admittedly selfishly, we were still going to have access to Nicklaus and get to watch him grow-up. It was a plan that was destined to be a win-win for everyone involved. The road of life can be filled with trials, challenges, and bumps for both humans and animals alike but it warms the cockles of the heart when so many adversities are overcome, culminating in happy endings. Little doubt that Nicklaus had a rough start in life but through seemingly divine intervention he miraculously landed strapped to a golden parachute.

It is still difficult to comprehend how quickly and deeply Nicklaus became so deep-seated in our hearts. It was becoming more and more unbearable to think he wasn't going to be around on a daily basis. I think David and Paula were becoming somewhat annoyed at how we were carrying-on but in all honesty, neither one of us could help ourselves.

Friday, December 30

I don't know how or why he was taking such a deep a hold on us. Perhaps it was our feeling of having saved this little guy from a certain early demise, or perhaps we needed to provide some good old fashion care and nurturing as much as Nicklaus needed it. We've always considered our pets as part of the family. As my mother was fond of saying, "dogs are people too," and that's pretty much our philosophy as well. In fact, we have a sign with those words on our back porch. Since we've always treated our two puppies as our children, I suppose it was inevitable that we'd look at Nicklaus as our third one and a tiny little baby to boot.

Nicklaus quickly had the run of the house and made himself at home.

Maybe it was the feeling of having truly rescued something from such a meager existence and certain extinction had we not had the fortune or more likely, divine intervention to make sure our paths had crossed. From that first cold, wet nose I felt embedded on my neck when I first scooped him up in my arms, there was such a deeply rooted connection I can only describe as truly magical. If magic really does exist, I believe I experienced it at it's best it right then and there.

We were both dreading this day, but still had to work through all the right reasons for giving Nick up for adoption. It was the right thing to do but even knowing that didn't make it any less difficult. Nick had stolen our hearts in a very short seven days like nothing or no one had ever done before. Had it just been me, I might have thought myself to be a sentimental old fool, but Nick had become embedded deeply within both my and Teresa's hearts.

Nicklaus spent the night before in his crate on the floor right beside the bed just like he had every night since Christmas Eve. Each night I tried to sleep with my arm dangling off the side of the bed and my hand close to Nick so he'd know I was right there. This morning we all slept until about 7:30, which was the longest Nick had made it through the night. But when my feet hit the floor, he was up and atom, ready to get out of that crate and head outdoors to do his business which he did with his usual predictability. When his feet hit the grass, he did his thing right on cue.

We were both beginning to sense just how difficult giving this little guy up was going to be but we also kept reassuring each other that it was the correct thing to do for all parties concerned. I think each time one of us began to think about it we became emotional about his departure. Each of us at separate times and both of us together would tear up over the thought. It was somewhat comforting to be able to tell each other that he wouldn't be far away and we would have visitation privileges pretty much as we liked or needed. We didn't know at the time just how true that statement would become over the months and years to follow.

We couldn't have asked for a better situation for Nicklaus to be accepted into than with Paula and David. They were so totally unselfish with sharing Nicklaus with us whenever we were in need of a "Nick-Fix." In fact here we were going to be dropping him off today December 30, 2005 and they had already invited us to dinner on New Year's Day. How thoughtful was that? Nicklaus would always have two sets of parents to love him, care for him, and to pamper him.

I didn't play golf that day so I could spend as much time as possible with him before we all took that drive through the country to deliver him to his new home.

Driving down the long driveway into Nick's new home, it's a wonder I didn't wipe out all the pasture fences and light poles framing the lane because my vision was blurred from the tears welling up in my eyes. I couldn't bear to look at Teresa with that little fuzz ball curdled up contently in her warm lap or we'd both lose it again. "We've got to be strong here," I kept thinking to myself. "We're doing the right thing." Again, the one saving grace was knowing we were always going to be able to see Nick, walk him or just play with him, but it wouldn't be the same since he was no longer "ours." I think we both knew what a wonderful companion he was destined to become, but we were going to play a much smaller role in his life from this point on. Maybe that's what made this moment so excruciatingly painful.

All puppies are cute and cuddly but this one had some special quality about him. It was as though he knew he had been rescued into something far greater than he could have ever imagined his life could become. He gushed so much love and appreciation out of his little body from the way he laid his head on your shoulder with that moist nose buried into the back of your neck, his floppy velveteen ears, the two white blazes on his nose and forehead and that warm fuzzy body. He just had the "it" factor oozing from his golden, glowing, fuzzy little self.

Friday, December 30

Nicklaus with his new Mother and new home.

I know dog trainers world-wide would have scolded me for allowing Nick to chew on my hands and fingers like I did, but as big a No-No as it is, it somehow pacified him and me as well to allow it. While my hands and fingers were scratched and cut from those razor sharp baby teeth, it didn't faze me in the least. I guess I looked at it as if he and I were bonding and I was certainly OK what that. I knew the purists of dogdom wouldn't approve but I was well aware we weren't going to be together forever so what he needed in terms of nurturing at that time in his young life, I was more than happy to give.

The hardest part was looking at my hands for days afterward and having an instant connection to the past six days with that little bundle of joy. We had become mesmerized as we watched him bouncing across the floor, or trying to pull the strands of lights off the Christmas tree, or suckling my thumb before falling asleep in my lap. Every scratch or scrape was well worth it.

As I've recanted a few of the other times in my life where I've had the opportunity to rescue animals from inevitable harm or even death, Nick's story is much more gratifying knowing the happy puppy he seemed to be and the fulfilled life that he was destine to experience. It was our good fortune that we were brought together if even for a short seven days. In the other cases, I had no further contact with the "rescued" again. I had no way of knowing if they found loving, caring homes, or even made it beyond puppyhood. We are blessed with the ability to see Nick and we can also appreciate that our actions on that Christmas Eve were just and right and all things good.

Whether it was fate, divine intervention or something in between, it was that spot in our heart for Nicklaus that still glows as brightly as it did during those treasured minutes, hours, and few short days that we shared with him. Our greatest gift is that he is still in our lives. It may not be on a daily basis but he lives just across town, so we often get the opportunity to see him, pet him, and share the joy and happiness in his life. He continues to provide joy to everyone around him with his charisma, gentle and caring personality, and an obvious gratefulness for the gift of life.

Friday, December 30

We will never forget him just as he has never forgotten us. His sense of smell and most likely our touch when we are around him seems to remind him of those seven days we spent together. It's like an old true friend who you haven't seen for some time but you know each other so well, you just pick back up where you left off. Almost as though you haven't been separated by time or miles and in your heart, you realize just how special such relationships are. We'll always cherish the love and nurturing that we managed to impart to one of God's special little creatures. One that we showered with as much tenderness, warmth, and care that we could over that short fortnight. We were then and always will be blessed by the opportunity to provide a chance at life for Nick and for the joy, love, and appreciation he shows to all those with whom he comes in contact.

I hope by now I've been able to instill in you the knowledge, belief that everyone should find that one diamond in the rough, that gem, that friend of a lifetime that is a one-in-a-million Dog. That one dog, like no other, that touches your soul with unconditional love and seers your heart with relentless joy. That one special animal that only God in his greatness could create and bless you with. So if you've had such a friend and companion, treasure those blessings for they are truly a gift of a lifetime. I've been doubly blessed along my path of life since Saint Nicklaus was my second such dog to fit that bill, even if it was for only a short seven mystical and magical days.

These were special moments with Nick.

Nicklaus grew into a stunningly beautiful, loving animal. It's hard to believe how many years it's been since we were blessed to find him, rescue him, and place him in a loving and caring home. He has became a family's (not just mans) best friend. From his adopted David and Paula to Nora, another adopted dog, to all their children and particularly, the grandchildren.

I saw David often at the golf club, and my usual first question was, "how's Nick?" Inevitably his response was, "he's so cute, wait till you hear what he did the other day." Then the conversation predictably proceeded to what person Nicklaus has fallen in love with or vice-versa. Nick's role in life seemed to be to please whomever

Friday, December 30

and however he could. As we certainly experienced, it was hard to not be smitten with his charm, personality, and the pure love that he shared to all.

David and Paula's granddaughter (Lilly) and Nicklaus became inseparable whenever she visited. Lilly and Nick had a love affair that rivals all those ever written about in the great literary works. Wherever Lilly went, Nick is close behind shadowing her every move.

Therein lies the essence of Nicklaus himself. His huge loving heart that has been and continues to be so incredibly giving. He came from nothing but gives everything to everyone; love, relentless affection, loyalty, and undying devotion. He filled our hearts and our minds with memories that should encompass a lifetime rather than a mere magical seven days. We were just so very blessed to be a small part of it!

Would I do it again? Rescue another one? Absolutely! If for no other reason than to experience the joy and love he brought to our lives in so short a time, but for the same enduring qualities he brought to David and Paula as well as the countless others lucky enough to have come in contact with him.

I Can't Wait to see what blessings await us down the road! I look forward to it!

Nicklaus fully grown. (Photo Paula Basher)

Postlogue

Nicklaus' life ended shortly before Thanksgiving 2019, at the age of fourteen.

Ever since that Christmas Eve of 2005, not a single Christmas has gone by that Nick wasn't at the fore front of my thoughts as our family prepared for and celebrated the season of our Lord and Savior's Birth. It was also the miracle of Nicklaus coming into our lives and blessing David and Paula as well as so many others. That day, the events and celebrations will always be a reminder of the Goodness and Grace of God for all his creations and for the bond of love between mankind and the creatures created by his skillful hands.

Thanks Be To God.

CPSIA information can be obtained
at www.ICGtesting.com
Printed in the USA
BVHW041631281221
625051BV00011B/1319